great songs... of the fifties

edited by milton okun

ISBN 1-57560-423-X

Visit our website at www.cherrylane.com

CONTENTS

INTRODUCTION

A wildly misperceived decade, the 1950s were never more so than when it came to music. As much as the era has become synonymous with the rise of the rebel rock 'n' roll, in reality the period was dominated by ballads popularized by already entrenched pop stars whose careers would continue and flourish at least until 1960. Dean Martin's "Memories Are Made of This," Frank Sinatra's "Young at Heart," "Three Coins in the Fountain" by the Four Aces, Eydie Gorme's version of "Fly Me to the Moon (In Other Words)," Nat King Cole's mellow "Too Young," and inspirational standards like "I Believe" and "Unchained Melody" were far more common and survived the years far better than the occasional raunchy R & B tune. One of the era's greatest R & B groups, in fact, was The Platters, whose smooth sound on "My Prayer," "Twilight Time," and "Only You (And You Alone)" more closely emulated forbearers like the Mills Brothers.

Moody, melodic or stirring, these ballads only emphasized how limited in emotional scope and variety the music of the fifties was, with many of the root forms like country music, blues, folk, R & B, Jamaican music, and jazz systematically eliminated from mass consideration. Though there was the occasional breakthrough of a "Sixteen Tons" or a "Singing the Blues" from the world of country music—the calypso inspired classics "Day-O (The Banana Boat Song)" and "Jamaica Farewell," the folk oriented "Kisses Sweeter Than Wine," written by members of The Weavers—it was this absence of diversity that paved the way for rock 'n' roll to expand from the underground by mixing genres into a simmering melting pot for the consumption of the new teen marketplace.

Here again, though, the image of rock 'n' roll as some sort of marauding force hell-bent on destroying the nation's youth, especially as seen through the perspective of fifty years, belies a far tamer reality. Apart from the limber Elvis Presley, many, if not most of the era's prime performers like Bobby Darin, Buddy Holly, Conway Twitty, and the Everly Brothers, were fairly upstanding, relatively sedate, conservative citizens. And if their individual fashion senses were a bit more radical than the prevailing crewcut norm, certainly the subject matter of their songs was as time honored and traditional as Tin Pan Alley ever got, excepting only that rock 'n' roll, being the first mass market music specifically designed for a teenage audience, featured more songs tailored to the special concerns of this group. So if pop music detailed a somewhat adult attitude about relationships, rock 'n' roll necessarily dwelt more heavily on songs of young love, primarily sung by guys, and written for girls.

The facts of teenage life being what they were, fantasy loves and unrequited loves were much more prevalent than the real type. Thus the preponderance in the early rock 'n' roll catalogue of songs like "Dream Lover," "All I Have to Do Is Dream," and "It's Only Make Believe." Usually the object of such ardor was an unattainable princess, elevated in song to scarifying heights, such as "Venus," or the more prosaic "Peggy Sue"; the subject of "Sixteen Candles" was less a specific celebrant than the magic age itself, at which time the dream girl emerged from her cocoon, an amalgam of all things svelte, pristine, and intoxicating. Even Elvis, despite his shimmy and his cowlick, was not immune to being victimized by this eternal 16-year-old female vixen, begging her to be gentle in "Don't Be Cruel (To a Heart That's True)" and "Love Me

Tender." But perhaps the more typical teenage boy posture was that of pining away unnoticed in the back of the class, or else the kind of bravado bordering on denial propagated by the horn-rimmed, angst-filled Crickets leader Buddy Holly in "That'll Be the Day" or The Platters in "The Great Pretender," summed up to vulnerable perfection by Carl Dobkins, Jr., in "My Heart Is an Open Book," a song which helped to launch the prolific pop career of lyricist Hal David.

All of which just serves to make Leiber & Stoller's savvy and brilliant "Kansas City" that much more of an enticing fantasy vision of heaven, where a fellow could bide his time on the corner of some mythical 12th Street and Vine, a bottle of port in one hand, and a luscious and available lady holding onto the other. Safe to say, few teenagers, boys or girls, ever got to live out this particular fantasy. If they were, like Elvis in "All Shook Up," a prisoner of the hormonal surges that would propel most of the best rock 'n' roll, they were also even more apt to be shackled by the weepy notions set forth by the pop crooner Johnny Mathis in "Misty" and "Wonderful Wonderful." More than anyone else, it is Mathis who may be held responsible for permanently mangling the emotional psyches of an entire generation with his remote take on passion; gorgeous as the tune of "Wonderful Wonderful" might be, its impossibly stirring climactic kiss would remain but a wistful dream destined to die unfulfilled for most of the millions of befuddled couples who tried to make out to *Johnny's Greatest Hits*, one of the top-selling albums of the entire decade.

If rock 'n' roll gave males any sense of self-esteem at all, it was when it celebrated its own exaggerated importance. It's no accident that "Rock Around the Clock" is generally regarded as one of the first defining moments of rock 'n' roll history. Introduced in the film *Blackboard Jungle*, its first impression has remained—that of a non-stop orgiastic party, where sheer attitude and endurance is of the highest value, animal energy triumphing over cerebral dating games. This rebellious stance that has trailed rock 'n' roll through the years has little to do with women and much more to do with male-on-male preening, aggression, and competition, like war games. When Carl Perkins is defending his "Blue Suede Shoes," it's not an incipient girlfriend he's talking to. And when Danny and his gang, The Juniors, detail the scene "At the Hop," seemingly a female domain, the song is less about learning how to dance than it is about *knowing the names* of all the dances, in this case knowing the names of *all the songs* about dances—the bop, the stroll, the slop, the calypso, the chicken (no one knew the actual steps to these dances; these dances didn't actually have steps anyway)—in other words, the statistics, like knowing the batting order of the 1957 Brooklyn Dodgers.

So whether it's the ballads or the bravado that got you through the 1950s, this is a book that will put it all back into your hands, with the opportunity to do it right this time.

Play on.

—Bruce Pollock

Deems Taylor Award–winning journalist Bruce Pollock is the author of three novels and seven books on popular music, including *The Rock Song Index*. He edits the annual reference book *Popular Music: An Annotated Index of American Popular Songs*.

All I Have to Do Is Dream

Words and Music by
Boudleaux Bryant

Moderately

Dream, _____ dream, dream, dream, _ Dream, _____ dream, dream, dream. _ When

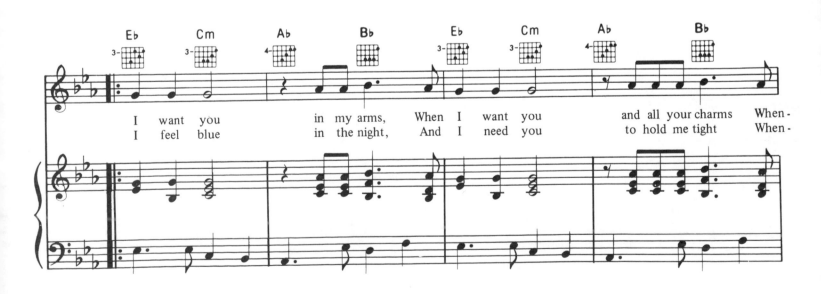

I want you in my arms, When I want you and all your charms When-
I feel blue in the night, And I need you to hold me tight When-

7

way! _____ I need you so that I could die, I love you so

and that is why When-ev-er I want you All I Have To Do Is

Dream. _____ Dream, _____

dream, dream, dream, __ Dream, _____ dream, dream, dream, __ dream.

rit.

8

All Shook Up

Words and Music by
Otis Blackwell and Elvis Presley

At the Hop

Words and Music by
Arthur Singer, John Madara
and David White

Ba ba ba ba, Ba ba ba ba, Ba ba ba ba, Ba ba ba ba, at the hop. Well, you can

Blue Suede Shoes

from G.I. BLUES

Words and Music by
Carl Lee Perkins

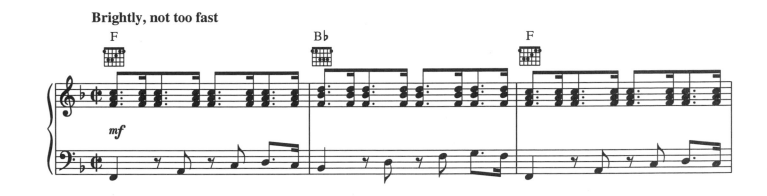

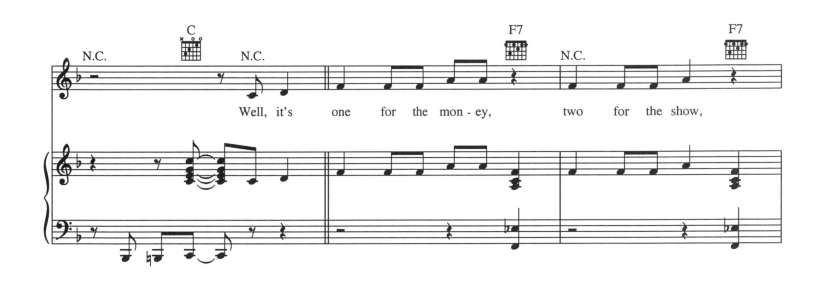

Well, it's one for the mon-ey, two for the show,

three to get read-y, now go, cat, go! But don't you

want to do, ___ but uh - uh, hon - ey, lay off of my shoes. ___ Don't you

step on my blue suede shoes.   You can

do an - y - thing ___ but lay off of my blue suede shoes. ___

___ Well, you can   shoes. ___

Catch a Falling Star

Words and Music by
Paul Vance and Lee Pockriss

21

Catch a fall-ing star and put it in your pock - et,

Nev - er let it fade a - way.

way. Catch a fall-ing star and put it in your pock - et.

Day-O
(The Banana Boat Song)

Words and Music by
Irving Burgie and William Attaway

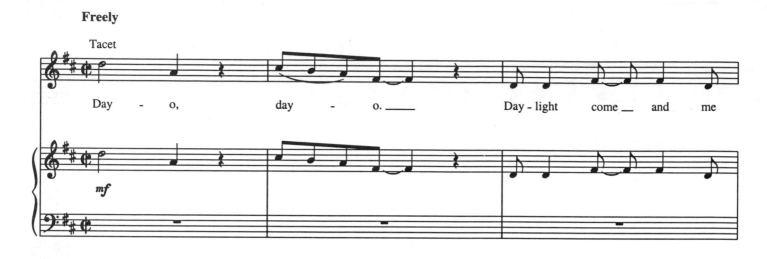

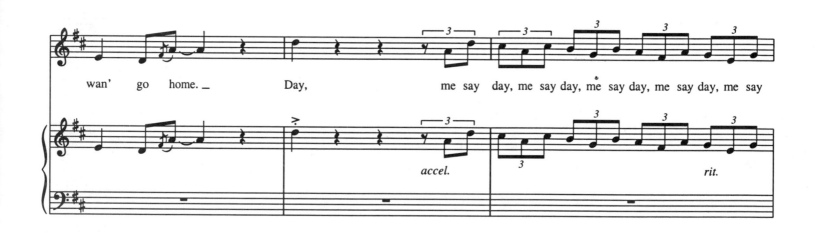

Moderate Calypso

Hide the dead-ly black ta-ran-t'la. Day-light come ___ and me

wan' go home. Day, me say day - o. ___

Day-light come ___ and me wan' go home. Day, me say,

day, me say day, me say... Day-light come ___ and me wan' go home.

28

Do-Re-Mi

from THE SOUND OF MUSIC

Lyrics by Oscar Hammerstein II

Music by Richard Rodgers

Allegretto

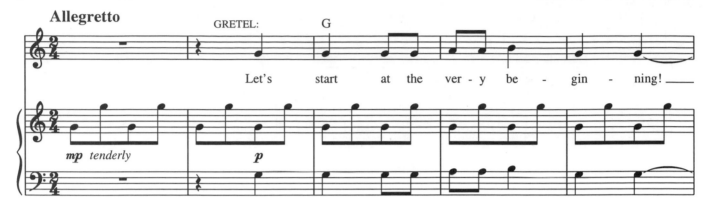

GRETEL: Let's start at the ver-y be-gin-ning! ___

MARIA: ___ A ver-y good place to start, ___ When you

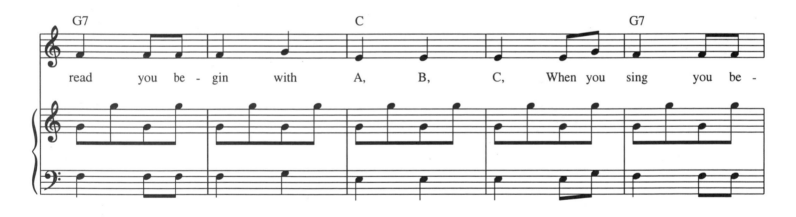

read you be-gin with A, B, C, When you sing you be-

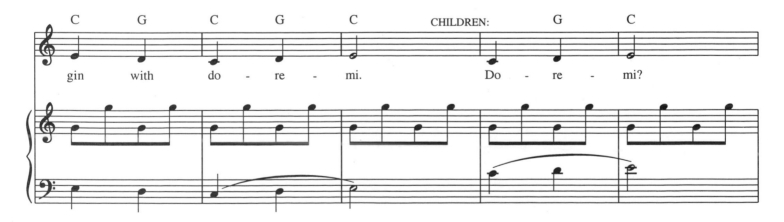

gin with do-re-mi. CHILDREN: Do-re-mi?

Don't Be Cruel
(To a Heart That's True)

Words and Music by
Otis Blackwell and Elvis Presley

Moderately, with half-time feel

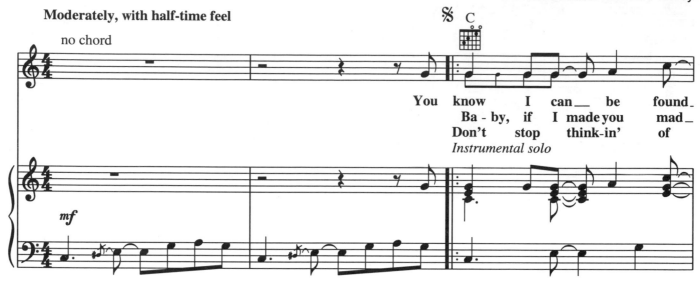

no chord

You know I can ___ be found ___
Ba - by, if I made you mad ___
Don't stop think - in' of
Instrumental solo

sit - tin' home all a - lone. ___
for some-thing I might have ___ said, ___
Don't make me feel this ___ way. ___
___ me.
If
Come

you can't come ___ a-round,
please let's for - get the past.
on o - ver here and love me.
at least please tel - e - phone. ___
The fu-ture looks bright a - head. ___
You know what I want you to

Dream Lover

Words and Music by
Bobby Darin

And a hand that I can hold _____ To feel you near when

I grow old?__ Be-cause I want _____ a girl _____ to

call _____ my own, _____ I want a dream lov-er so

I don't have to dream a-lone._____

Some day, I don't know how, _____ I hope you'll

hear my plea. _____ Some way, I don't know how, _____

She'll bring her love to me. _____ Dream lov-er,

un-til then _____ I'll go to sleep and dream a-gain. _____

Fly Me to the Moon
(In Other Words)
featured in the Motion Picture ONCE AROUND

Words and Music by
Bart Howard

47

The Great Pretender

Words and Music by
Buck Ram

yes,__ I'm the great pre-tend-er,__ A-drift in a world__ of my

own; I play the game__ but, to my real shame, You've

left me to dream__ all a-lone, Too real __ is this feel-ing of

make-be-lieve, Too real ____ when I feel ____ what my

Honeycomb

Words and Music by
Bob Merrill

Additional Lyrics

2. Now have you heard tell how they made a bee?
   Then tried a hand at a green, green tree.
   So the tree was made and I guess you've heard,
   Next they made a bird.
   Then they went around lookin' everywhere,
   Takin' love from here and from there,
   And they stored it up in a little cart,
   For my honey's heart.
   Chorus

I Believe

Words and Music by
Ervin Drake, Irvin Graham,
Jimmy Shirl and Al Stillman

Moderately (with much expression)

I Be-lieve for ev-'ry drop of rain that falls,_____ a flow-er

grows._____ I Be-lieve that some-where in the

dark-est night,_____ a can-dle glows._____

Hot Diggity
(Dog Ziggity Boom)

Words and Music by
Al Hoffman and Dick Manning

59

I'm Gonna Sit Right Down and Write Myself a Letter

from AIN'T MISBEHAVIN'

Lyric by Joe Young

Music by Fred E. Ahlert

Jamaica Farewell

Words and Music by
Irving Burgie

on my way, ___ Won't be back for

man - y a day. My heart is down, ___ my head is

turn - ing a - round, ___ I had to leave a lit - tle crab in

King - ston town. ___

It's Only Make Believe

Words and Music by
Conway Twitty and Jack Nance

Peo - ple see us ev - 'ry - where __ they think you real - ly care, __

but my - self I can't de - ceive, I know it's on - ly make be -

lieve.

My one and on - ly prayer is that some - day you'll care, __

my hopes, my dreams come true, my one and on - ly you,

no one will ev - er know, __ how much I love you so,

my on - ly prayer will be, some - day you'll care for me, but it's

on - ly__ make __ be -

my plans, my hopes, my schemes, you are my ev - 'ry - thing, but it's
my on - ly prayer will be that some - day you'll care for me but it's

on - ly _____ make _____ be -
on - ly _____ make _____ be -

lieve. _____

lieve. _____

69

Kansas City

from SMOKEY JOE'S CAFE

Words and Music by
Jerry Leiber and Mike Stoller

crazy way of lov-in' there and I'm gon-na get me some.

I'm gon-na be stand-in' on the cor-ner___ Twelfth Street and Vine.
pack___ my clothes,___ leave at the___ crack of dawn.

I'm gon-na be
I'm go-in' to

might take a train, _____ I might take a plane, _____ but
stay with that wom - an _____ I know I'm gon - na die, _____ got - ta

if I have to walk _____ I'm goin' just the same. _____ I'm go - in' to
find a brand new ba - by _____ and that's the rea - son why I'm go - in' to

Kan - sas Cit - y, _____ Kan - sas Cit - y here I

come. _____ They got a

cra - zy way of lov - in' there and I'm gon - na get me some.

I'm go - in' to

They got a cra - zy way of lov - in' there and

I'm gon - na get me some.

Lollipop

Words and Music by
Beverly Ross and Julius Dixon

With a beat

Lol - li - pop, lol - li - pop, Oh,_____ lol - li, lol - li, lol - li, lol - li - pop, lol - li - pop, Oh,__ _____ lol - li, lol - li, lol - li, lol - li - pop, lol - li - pop, Oh,_____ lol - li, lol - li, lol - li, lol - li - pop.

Call my ba - by lol - li - pop,
Cra - zy way she thrills - a me,

Kisses Sweeter Than Wine

Words by
Ronnie Gilbert, Lee Hays,
Fred Hellerman and Pete Seeger

Music by Huddie Ledbetter

Slowly, but with a steady beat

Chorus

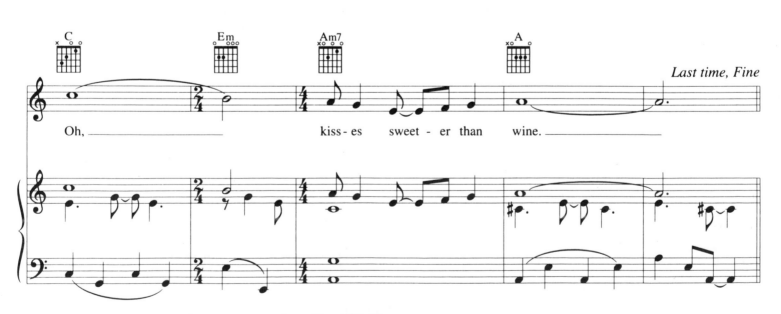

Verse 2:
He asked me to marry and be his sweet wife,
And we would be so happy all of our life.
He begged and he pleaded like a natural man and then,
Oh, Lord, I gave him my hand. *(Repeat chorus)*

Verse 3:
I worked mighty hard and so did my wife,
A-workin' hand in hand to make a good life.
With corn in the fields and wheat in the bins and then,
Oh, Lord, I was the father of twins. *(Repeat chorus)*

Verse 4:
Our children numbered just about four
And they all had sweethearts knock on the door.
They all got married and they didn't wait, I was,
Oh, Lord, the grandfather of eight. *(Repeat chorus)*

Verse 5:
Now we are old and ready to go
We get to thinkin' what happened a long time ago.
We had lots of kids and trouble and pain, but,
Oh, Lord, we'd do it again. *(Repeat chorus)*

Love Me Tender

from LOVE ME TENDER

Words and Music by
Elvis Presley and Vera Matson

life com - plete, and I love you so.
I be - long, and we'll nev - er part.
all the years till the end of time.
fol - low you ev - 'ry - where you go.

Love me ten - der, love me true, all my dreams ful -

fill. For, my dar - lin', I love you,

and I al - ways will. and I al - ways will.

Luck Be a Lady
from GUYS AND DOLLS

By Frank Loesser

Lady to - night.____

Luck, let a gen - tle - man see ____

How nice a dame you can be ____

I know the way you've treat-ed oth-er guys you've been with Luck Be A

84

Lady with me. _____ A

la - dy does - n't leave her es - cort _____ It is - n't

fair _____ It is - n't nice! _____ A

la - dy does - n't wan - der all ov - er the room and

blow on some oth - er guy's dice. _____ So,

May You Always

Words and Music by
Larry Markes and Dick Charles

Memories Are Made of This

Words and Music by
Richard Dehr, Frank Miller
and Terry Gilkyson

93

One man, one wife, one love thru life.

Mem - o - ries are made of this___

Mem - o - ries are made of this.___

95

Misty

Words by Johnny Burke

Music by Erroll Garner

My Heart Is an Open Book

Lyric by Hal David

Music by Lee Pockriss

Look!   My heart is an o - pen book.

My   love   is hon - est and

true.   Some jeal - ous so and so   wants us to

part.   That's why {he's she's} tell - in' you   that I've got a

cheat-in' heart. Don't be-lieve all those lies dar-lin' just be-

lieve your eyes and Look! Look! My heart is an

o - pen book. I love

no-bod-y but you. you.

My Prayer

Music by Georges Boulanger
Lyric and Musical Adaptation by Jimmy Kennedy

Only You

(And You Alone)

Words and Music by
Buck Ram and Ande Rand

Peggy Sue
from THE BUDDY HOLLY STORY

Words and Music by
Jerry Allison, Norman Petty
and Buddy Holly

Very brightly

If you knew_____ Peg - gy Sue,_____ Then you'd
Peg - gy Sue,_____ Peg - gy Sue,_____ Oh, how

know why I feel blue_____ A - bout Peg - gy,_____
my heart yearns for you,_____ Oh, Pa - heg - gy,_____

'Bout my Peg - gy Sue;_____
My Pa - heg - gy Sue;_____

Oh, well, I love you, gal,_____ Yes, I love you, Peg - gy Sue:_____

Peg - gy Sue,_____

Peg - gy Sue,_____ Pret - ty, pret - ty, pret - ty, pret - ty,

Peg - gy Sue,_____ Oh, my Peg - gy,_____ My

Rock Around the Clock

Words and Music by
Max C. Freedman and Jimmy DeKnight

Sea of Love

Words and Music by
George Khoury and Philip Baptiste

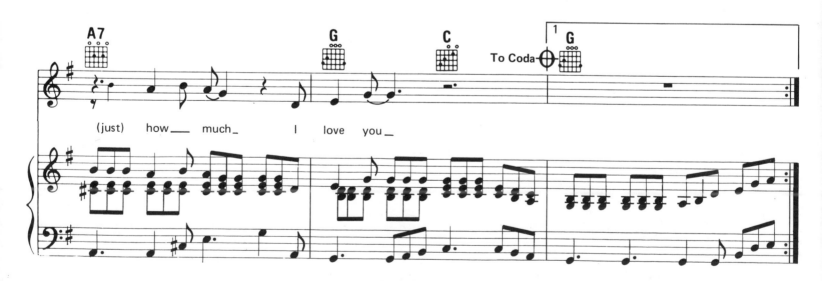

Come _____ with me _____

to _____ the sea _____ of love. _____

D.C. al Coda
(verse 1)

CODA

Guitar Tacet

Come _____ with me _____

to _____ the sea _____ of

115

love._____ Come with me___ my___ love_

to the sea,_____ the sea___ of love._ I ___ want to tell you

just how__ much I love you._

I ___ want to tell you, oh,__ how much_ I love you.

rit.

116

Secretly

Words and Music by
Al Hoffman, Dick Manning
and Mark Markwell

See You in September

Words by Sid Wayne

Music by Sherman Edwards

see you _____ when the sum-mer's through. _____

Here we are, say - ing good - bye at the

sta - tion, _____ sum - mer va - ca - tion _____

_____ is tak - ing you a - way. _____ Have a

good time, _____ but re - mem - ber _____ there is

dan - ger _____ in the sum-mer moon a - bove. _____

___ Will I see you _____ in Sep -

To Coda ⊕

tem - ber, _____ or lose you _____

Silhouettes

Words and Music by
Frank C. Slay Jr. and Bob Crewe

Put {his/her} arms a-round your waist, held you tight, kiss-es I could al-most taste in the night, Won-dered why I'm not the {guy/girl} whose sil-hou-ette's on the shade I could-n't hide the tears in my eyes Ah, _____

Lost con-trol, and rang your bell, I was sore, "Let me in, or else I'll

beat down your door." When two stran-gers, who had been two sil-hou-ettes on the

shade said to my shock, "You're on the wrong block." Rushed down to your house with

wings on my feet, Loved you like I've nev-er loved you my

Singing the Blues

Words and Music by
Melvin Endsley

cry _____ o - ver you___ well, I nev - er felt more like

run - ning a - way___ but why should I go ___ 'cause I could - n't stay___ with -

out you. You got me sing - ing the blues. _____

Well, I blues. _____

Standing on the Corner

from THE MOST HAPPY FELLA

By Frank Loesser

that got the cream,
and I'm so broke,

Have-n't got a girl,___
Could-n't buy a girl,___

But I can dream,
a nick-el coke,

Have-n't got a girl,___
Still I'm liv-ing like___

But I can wish, so I
A mil-lion-aire, when I

take me down to Main Street And
take me down to Main Street And

that's where I se-lect my i-mag-i-na-ry dish!
I re-view the ha-rem pa-rad-ing for me there.

D.S. al Coda
(1st verse)

CODA

by.___

Sixteen Candles

Words and Music by
Luther Dixon and Allyson R. Khent

Sixteen Tons

Words and Music by
Merle Travis

Chorus

mind ___ that's ___ weak ___ and a back that's strong. You load
straw - boss ___ said ___ "Well - a bless my soul." You load
high - toned ___ wo - man make me walk the line. You load

Six - teen Tons,

what do you get? ___ An - oth - er day old - er and deep - er in debt. ___ Saint

Pe - ter, don't you call me 'cause I can't go ___ I owe ___ my soul to the

com - pa - ny store. ___

2. I was
3. I was
4. If you

Suddenly There's a Valley

Words and Music by
Chuck Meyer and Biff Jones

Take the "A" Train

Words and Music by
Billy Strayhorn

rid - ing. _____ That's where___ ro-mance may be

hid - ing. _____ For - get _____ your car or

air-plane. _____ You'll find that it -'ll pay to take the

"A" train. _____ "A" train. _____

Three Coins in the Fountain

Words by Sammy Cahn

Music by Jule Styne

each heart long - ing for its home,   there they lie in the

foun - tain   some - where in the heart of Rome.

Which one will the foun - tain bless?   Which one will the foun - tain

bless?   Three coins in the foun - tain,

That'll Be the Day

Words and Music by
Jerry Allison, Norman Petty
and Buddy Holly

Moderately with a Beat

Well, you give me all your lov-in' and your tur-tle-dov-in', All____ your hugs an' kiss-es an' your mon-ey too;____ Well,

you know you love me, ba-by, Un-til you tell me, may-be, that some day, well, I'll be through! Well,____

That-'ll Be The Day, when you say, good-bye, Yes,____ That-'ll Be The Day, when

Too Young

Words by Sylvia Dee

Music by Sid Lippman

Turn Around

Words and Music by
Alan Greene, Malvina Reynolds
and Harry Belafonte

26 Miles
(Santa Catalina)

Words and Music by
Glen Larson and Bruce Belland

Moderate Rock tempo

Twen - ty six miles a - cross the sea ___

San - ta Ca - ta - li - na is a - wait - in' for me, ___ San - ta Ca - ta - li - na, the

is - land of ___ ro - mance, _ ro - mance, _ ro - mance, _ ro - mance. _ Wa - ter all a - round it

ev - 'ry - where, _ trop - i - cal trees and the salt - y air; _ but for

me the thing that's a - wait - in' there's _ ro - mance. _

It seems so dis - tant, twen - ty - six miles _ a - way,
trop - i - cal heav - en out in the o - cean

rest - in' in the wa - ter se - rene. _ I'd work for an - y - one,
cov - ered with trees and girls. _ If I have to swim _ I'd

even the Na - vy, who would float me to my is - land dream. __
do it for - ev - er till I'm gaz - in' on those is - land pearls. __

Twen - ty - six miles, so near yet far. _____ I'd
For - ty kil - o - me - ters in a leak - y old boat, ___

swim with just some wa - ter wings and my gui - tar. _____ I can
an - y old _____ thing that - 'll stay a - float. ___ When _____

leave the wings but I'll need the gui - tar _____ for ro - mance, __
we ar - rive we'll _____ all _____ pro - mote _____ ro - mance, __

154

Twilight Time

Lyric by Buck Ram

Music by Morty Nevins and Al Nevins

Unchained Melody
from the Motion Picture UNCHAINED

Lyric by
Hy Zaret

Music by
Alex North

much, are you still mine? _____ I

need your love, _____ I need your love, _____ God

speed your love _____ to me! _____

Lone - ly riv - ers flow _____ to the sea, _____ to the
Lone - ly moun - tains gaze _____ at the stars, _____ at the

When

Words and Music by
Jack Reardon and Paul Evans

When, when you smile,— when you smile— at me,—

well, well, I know— our love will al - ways be.—

When, when you kiss,— when you kiss— me right,—

I, I don't want— to ev - er say good-night.—

I need you, I want you near me.

I love you, yes I do, and I hope you hear me

when, when I say,—— when I say,—— "Be mine."——

If, if you will—— I know all will be fine.——

—— When will you be

mine? mine?——

Venus

Words and Music by
Edward Marshall

Hey, Ve - nus, ____ oh, Ve - nus.

Hey, Ve - nus,

Ve - nus, if you will, please send a lit - tle girl for me to thrill,

Wonderful! Wonderful!

Words by Ben Raleigh

Music by Sherman Edwards

won - der - ful! won - der - ful!

won - der - ful! won - der - ful!

Oh, so won-der-ful, my love!

Oh, so won-der-ful, my love!

This world is full of won - d'rous things, it's

true, but they would-n't have much mean-ing with - out you.

Some qui-et eve - nings I sit by your side and we're lost in a world of our

Young at Heart

Words by Carolyn Leigh

Music by Johnny Richards

More Great Piano/Vocal Books from Cherry Lane

For a complete listing of Cherry Lane titles available,
including contents listings, please visit our web site at
www.cherrylane.com

02500343	Almost Famous	$16.95
02501801	Amistad	$14.95
02502171	The Best of Boston	$17.95
02500144	Mary Chapin Carpenter – Party Doll	$16.95
02502163	Mary Chapin Carpenter – Stones in the Road	$17.95
02502165	John Denver Anthology – Revised	$22.95
02505512	Best of John Denver for Easy Piano	$9.95
02503629	Best of John Denver – Piano Solos	$10.95
02502227	John Denver – A Celebration of Life	$14.95
02500002	John Denver Christmas	$14.95
02502166	John Denver's Greatest Hits	$17.95
02502151	John Denver – A Legacy in Song (Softcover)	$24.95
02502152	John Denver – A Legacy in Song (Hardcover)	34.95
02500326	John Denver – The Wildlife Concert	$17.95
02509922	The Songs of Bob Dylan	$29.95
02500175	Linda Eder – It's No Secret Anymore	$14.95
02502209	Linda Eder – It's Time	17.95
02509912	Erroll Garner Songbook, Vol. 1	$17.95
02500270	Gilbert & Sullivan for Easy Piano	$12.95
02500318	Gladiator	$12.95
02500273	Gold & Glory: The Road to El Dorado	$14.95
02502126	Best of Guns N' Roses	$17.95
02502072	Guns N' Roses – Selections from Use Your Illusion I and II	$17.95
02500014	Sir Roland Hanna Collection	$19.95
02502134	Best of Lenny Kravitz	$12.95
02500012	Lenny Kravitz – 5	$16.95
02502201	The Songs of David Mallett – A Collection	$17.95
02500003	Dave Matthews Band – Before These Crowded Streets	$17.95
02502199	Dave Matthews Band – Crash	$17.95
02502192	Dave Matthews Band – Under the Table and Dreaming	$17.95
02500081	Natalie Merchant – Ophelia	$14.95
02502204	The Best of Metallica	$17.95
02500010	Tom Paxton – The Honor of Your Company	$17.95
02507962	Peter, Paul & Mary – Holiday Concert	$17.95
02500145	Pokemon 2.B.A. Master	$9.95
02500026	The Prince of Egypt	$16.95
02502189	The Bonnie Raitt Collection	$22.95
02502230	Bonnie Raitt – Fundamental	$17.95
02502139	Bonnie Raitt – Longing in Their Hearts	$16.95
02502088	Bonnie Raitt – Luck of the Draw	$14.95
02507958	Bonnie Raitt – Nick of Time	$14.95
02502190	Bonnie Raitt – Road Tested	$24.95
02502218	Kenny Rogers – The Gift	$16.95
02500072	Saving Private Ryan	$14.95
02500197	SHeDAISY – The Whole SHeBANG	$14.95
02500166	Steely Dan – Anthology	$17.95
02500284	Steely Dan – Two Against Nature	$14.95
02500165	Best of Steely Dan	$14.95
02502132	Barbra Streisand – Back to Broadway	$19.95
02507969	Barbra Streisand – A Collection: Greatest Hits and More	$17.95
02502164	Barbra Streisand – The Concert	$22.95
02502228	Barbra Streisand – Higher Ground	$16.95
02500196	Barbra Streisand – A Love Like Ours	$16.95
02503617	John Tesh – Avalon	$15.95
02500128	Best of John Tesh (EZ Play Today)	$8.95
02502178	The John Tesh Collection	$17.95
02503623	John Tesh – A Family Christmas	$15.95
02505511	John Tesh – Favorites for Easy Piano	$9.95
02503630	John Tesh – Grand Passion	$15.95
02500124	John Tesh – One World	$14.95
02500307	John Tesh – Pure Movies 2	$14.95
02502175	Tower of Power – Silver Anniversary	$17.95
02502198	The "Weird Al" Yankovic Anthology	$17.95
02502217	Trisha Yearwood – A Collection of Hits	$16.95
02500334	Maury Yeston – December Songs	$17.95
02502225	The Maury Yeston Songbook	$19.95

See your local music dealer or contact:

CHERRY LANE MUSIC COMPANY
6 East 32nd Street, New York, NY 10016

EXCLUSIVELY DISTRIBUTED BY

HAL•LEONARD® CORPORATION
7777 W. BLUEMOUND RD. P.O. BOX 13819 MILWAUKEE, WI 53213

Prices, contents and availability subject to change without notice.